The Shelby Trained Code

Simple Strategies to Successfully Change Your Health, Fitness, and Life

Shelby R. Turcotte

LEGAL NOTICE

PRAISE AND PROMOTION FOR
THE SHELBY TRAINED CODE

The Shelby Trained Code *not only helped me to lose the weight gained with transition into mid-life, but also to feel the strongest I have ever felt without injury or sacrificing flexibility or endurance. The methodologies have proved to be invaluable to my overall physical and mental health.*
- Dr. Cathy Jakubowitch

The Shelby Trained Code *is a calculated approach to training based off of nearly 14 years of working with athletes like myself. Do yourself a favor and follow the advice contained in here.*
- Isaac Lipton, Former Division 1 Lacrosse Player

Why should you follow the advice in The Shelby Trained Code *to help you achieve your goals? My answer is simple: Few people have the drive, meticulous attention to detail, and desire to innovate that Shelby so effortlessly exudes.*
- Ben Coleman, Former College Baseball Player

I wouldn't have gained the same confidence in my body without the help and guidance of Shelby and his methods contained in this book. My only regret was that I wished I had this book when I started training.
- Olivia Leavitt, Former College Tennis Player

DEDICATION

This book is dedicated to the hundreds of clients whom I've been able to coach, interact with, and learn from over the last 14 years. I appreciate the trust you've given me and those around me to help you reach your goals. I hope that this book helps to inspire you to continue making positive changes in your life and help impact those around you. Here's to a happy, healthy, and enjoyable life – one day at a time.

ACKNOWLEDGEMENTS

During my junior year in college I took an internship at a gym to learn about the business of running a health and fitness club. During that time I was able to shadow a personal trainer named Cathy Woodhouse. That experience led me to take a job as a personal trainer a year later and ultimately led to a career in the fitness industry. Over the last 14 years I've spent hours learning from the best minds in the industry.

Thank you to John Brubaker and Pat Rigsby. Your business knowledge, professional approach, and insight have allowed me to build a business that I'm proud of. Without you two pushing me this book wouldn't have been written. Thank you, Mike Boyle – who shared his knowledge and wisdom countless times expecting nothing in return. Industry leaders like Dan John, Eric Cressey, Mike Robertson, Gray Cook, John Berardi, Stuart McGill, and Ben Bruno – I've watched, read, and learned from your experiences more than you'd ever realize.

My first book wouldn't be complete without thanking my parents for the qualities they've instilled in me as a person and professional. Kayla, thank you for pushing the brand to new heights. I want to thank my daughters (Teagan and Isla) for sharing their daddy many early mornings, late nights, and weekends. Lastly, I want to thank my wife, Heather. The sacrifices she's made in her life to allow me to build the Shelby Trained brand can't be overstated. Without her, you wouldn't be reading this.

INTRODUCTION

What you hold in your hands are the most powerful strategies that someone can implement to create positive change in life. My goal with this book was to compile the most simple and effective tips that I've learned over the years from being in the trenches. It's part science and part art, but all with the end goal of creating change in your "real" life.

In a day and age when technology and social media continue to create the belief that change occurs with a simple "click" of a button, I am constantly reminding people that lasting change is the result of a number of small decisions, habits, and patterns that, when done consistently with a high level of effort, change lives. Not only their own, but those around them too. I have reminded successful clients on a handful of occasions that *you too are an inspiration to those you interact with on a regular basis.* They look up to you and want to learn how you did "it." My hope is that this book helps spark the behavioral change needed to enhance the quality of your life on a daily basis, whether it be moving pain-free, climbing a mountain, losing fat, or playing sports.

*Disclaimer: These rules are not a substitute for advice or consultation with a physician, dietician, psychologist, psychiatrist, or other medical professional. **By the way kids, the <u>italicized rules</u> are for entertainment purposes only.**

TABLE OF CONTENTS

Rule #1
Your body is not falling apart because of your age.

This is the very first rule for a very good reason. I see many people who blame their issues on their age.

Upon having our first child in 2012 I began taking more adults on as private clients. As my business evolved, I began to carve out a niche with people who wanted to live active lifestyles but had restrictions as a result of orthopedic issues (knees, hips, shoulders, back, etc.).

It's not your age.

Your body is falling apart because of the cumulative wear and tear from "life." Of course it accumulates over time, but the reality is I've seen athletes who are young but "used" their body hard and have the issues to show for it; and I've seen adults who've been much more conservative with their body and have years left that they often don't realize.

Bottom line: Age ain't nothin' but a number.

Rule #2
You should be making progress until you're at least 85.

My daily interactions with clients ages 50-82 have changed my perspective on what the body is capable of doing. I'm now convinced that not only can clients maintain their health and fitness, but they can improve the quality of their movement, strength, and stability at a much greater rate than previously thought.

Not only can you get back to a "baseline" level of function after an injury/issue; you can far surpass that!

Bottom line: Start sooner rather than later, but don't stop.

Rule #3
Frequency matters more than (almost) anything.

If it matters, do it more. I'm regularly trying to convince people that intensity often matters a great deal less, but how often you do something matters more.

The most powerful part of this statement is that I've seen it work in all aspects of life: fitness, nutrition, business, even relationships.

Bottom line: You're almost always better off reducing intensity and increasing the frequency.

Rule #4
Once you stop chasing results, they start to magically happen.

Much like people chasing jobs to make more money, in fitness people often chase the numbers (scale, weights, tests) thinking they'll improve their results. Spend more time focusing on the underlying actions that drive the goal and less time on the goal itself. The best way to do this is to have a plan:

- If it's weight loss, maybe the goal is to hit your daily caloric intake 6 out of 7 days.
- If it's regain activity, maybe that means doing 5-10 minutes each day of movement/mobility work.
- If it's to get faster, maybe that means you're working on 3-5 drills each day before practice.

Bottom line: Stop weighing yourself every day, thinking about what you can't do, or comparing yourself to others. Instead, focus on the daily actions.

Warm-Up/Prehab:

The training before the training...

Rule #5
Myth: Static stretching makes you more flexible.

Fact: Full range-of-motion strength movements are the single best thing you can do for flexibility. By taking a muscle(s) through a range of motion (movement), under load (lifting a weight), you are effectively restructuring the muscles (tissue) at the new length.

Can't get on and off of a couch without leaning over? Improve your squats – go lower, get stronger, and watch your legs, hips, and knees improve.

In addition, doing so has the best long-term effect as far as holding muscle length.

Rule #6
No one cares if you can touch your toes.

Focus on developing range of motion that is useful, not just "flexibility." Touching your toes doesn't necessarily help you do much except brush dirt off your shoes. The question is, can you pick up a box/bag/item off the floor and safely get it to where it needs to go?

Rule #7
I don't hate stretching.

Stretches never did anything bad to me or my family. I have nothing against them. I just believe that most people blindly start doing them thinking stretching will solve their problem(s):

- Prevent injury
- Reduce pain
- File their taxes, etc.

Static stretches (passively holding a stretch for a period of time – think old-school hurdle stretch) are useful as part of the "big picture." In particular, I think they are effective when used early in the workout (after foam rolling to have more motion) or after a workout (to get muscles to relax).

Rule #8
Don't spend 10 minutes stretching.

If you're spending 10 minutes stretching before a workout and your goal is to lose 30lbs, you have it all wrong. There are really only three stretches most people need to do:

- Hip flexor/quad stretch
- Hamstrings stretch
- Wall triceps.

Your hips will be looser. Your back will feel better. And your posture will be much improved. Hold each stretch for about 30 seconds each side and then move on with life.

Rule #9
Why are you stretching?

Before you start stretching, ask yourself why. Stretching to "get more flexible" without a purpose is useless. "To prevent injury" isn't a good reason either. There is minimal to no (good) research that supports static stretching reduces your risk of injury or reduces pain.

Why are you still doing it? Good question. Figure out what you're trying to get from the stretching and then figure out if/how doing it best matches your goals. If you can't answer that question, hire someone who can.

Rule #10
Move every 45 minutes.

If you have a desk job, set a timer, get up and do the exact opposite of what you do when you sit. Reach overhead, reach back, move side to side, use one leg at a time, and work your upper back.

If you stand a lot, set a timer, and do the exact opposite of what you do when you stand: Squat, bend over, reach overhead, and use one leg at a time.

For years everyone thought we were sitting too much. The answer – stand. Then as people stood more and saw issues, the answer was to sit.

Today's answer: Don't stay in the same position for an extended period of time. Move.

Rule #11
Do no more than 3 stretches regularly.

If you're doing more than 3 stretches on a regular basis, you should take a look at the training program you are following. (Hint: It's not working.)

A proper training program will develop flexibility and extensibility in the tissues throughout the body. I often hear from clients that despite the fact we don't stretch (much), they get more flexible.

Wondering what 3 stretches you should do? If you don't know, the 3 stretches most people need to do: hip flexor/quad stretch, hamstrings stretch, and wall triceps. For those who sit a lot, these 3 should be your go-to stretches.

Rule #12
Dynamic warm-ups are the best short warm-up.

Dynamic warm ups are the single most effective way for you to move and feel better with the least amount of stress and the most reward. Dynamic warm-ups should move the body through all planes of motion while enhancing all major patterns of the body.

A sample dynamic warm-up that can be used prior to training: high knees, butt kicks, lunges, lateral lunges, step-behinds, toe touches, shuffles, carioca.

NOTE: See video example:
shelbytrained.com/thecode

Rule #13
Make sure baby got back.

Use your butt.

The lifeblood of the body is the booty. Everything from back pain and knee problems to jumping higher and running faster is dictated in large part by the peaches on your backside. Warm them up so they function properly every workout.

Two great choices:

- Lateral band walks
- Hip lifts/bridges.

Spend a couple of minutes making sure these things burn. You'll thank me later.

NOTE: See video example:
shelbytrained.com/thecode

Rule #14
The 2 upper-body muscles you must train (that you've never heard of):

Lower and middle traps. Whether you want to bench more, squat more, improve your posture, reduce back pain (or all of the above), the lower and middle traps should be trained more often than you change your socks.

No idea what I'm talking about? That's a good sign that you're not training them. The good news for you: I've got some video demonstrations for you at shelbytrained.com/thecode.

Have some idea what I'm talking about? Start with prone or seated Ys and work up to prone military press and wall-trace variations. A couple sets of 10-15 reps should be sufficient.

Rule #15
Do what you hate first.

Warm-ups are a great place for you to put movements that matter but that you don't want to do – i.e., mobility work (think moving more flexible), small-muscle movements (not arms and abs), etc. This works wonders for multiple reasons:

1) You can do them when you're still focused and not fatigued (quality is higher).
2) You are less likely to skip them.
3) They generally help you have a more productive workout by preparing your body for what you're about to do.

Don't make it complicated – the more you hate it, the earlier in your workout you should do it.

Rule #16
Have your warm-up written down.

Write down your warm-up. As ridiculous as it sounds, you're more likely to follow a routine that is down on paper/phone/etc. If you don't have it written down, it's much easier to justify skipping over it.

If you need a sample warm-up, see: shelbytrained.com/thecode

Rule #17
Timed warm-ups can be your friend.

If you're like me and you hate warming up, try the "timed warm-up" method:

Set a timer on your phone for 3-5 minutes. Now move through those movements non-stop for that period of time. Now go work out.

If you struggle with what you should do: split squats, push-ups, single-leg toe touches, prone Ts, and supine leg holds.

NOTE: If you're looking for video examples, visit shelbytrained.com/thecode.

Strength / Resistance Training:

Rule #18
Skip traditional crunches.

Your abdominal muscles are tethers/anchors for your torso. Train them to resist movement and control movement more than create it. Use a variety of movements to develop this:

- Planks
- Side planks
- Carries – anything that helps train the core to resist movement first is usually a good thing!

NOTE: For video examples, visit shelbytrained.com/thecode.

Rule #19
There is no 12oz dumbbell.

Despite what my clients tell me, I have yet to see an actual 12oz weight for curls. Even more worrisome is that it seems to make their stomachs bigger and not their arms...

Rule #20
The rule of one:
1 always comes before 2

If you're looking to increase both function and strength, using one limb (arm, leg) at a time in a strength movement is almost always the better choice. It increases coordination and core development, and points out imbalances in your body.

Rule #21
Bench pressing to failure will only make you one.

I once had an athlete tell me that he went home, took pre-workout (to get energy), proceeded to put 60 additional pounds on the bar (to bench), and wanted to see if he could lift it.

The answer was no.

Ten minutes after he crawled out from underneath the barbell, he realized you improve strength by actually lifting it – not "trying" to lift it.

*See Rule #22.

Rule #22
Don't "try" to see if you can lift a weight.

Putting a weight on the bar and seeing if you can lift it is like taking a test: It simply shows how much strength/power you have right now; it doesn't train it.

I see far too many people (i.e., athletes) put weight on a bar and "try to lift it." That's like taking a test without increasing your knowledge. Instead, spend the time improving your knowledge and magically the test becomes much easier.

Bottom line: Only "test" your knowledge (strength) 2-3 times per year – if at all.

Rule #23
Do more of what you hate.

Hate an exercise? You should probably do more of it. It typically means that you're not good at it. "Not good at it" typically means that you lack mobility, stability, strength, or confidence. Any, or all, of the previous are "OK" and they simply mean that you should address the weakness.

Rule #24
Don't worry about rule #23; soon you'll find a new exercise that you hate even more.

As people progress over time, we're continually finding new ways to challenge them. That means that soon there will be a new variation/exercise/piece of equipment to dream about.

Rule #25
Filling your pockets with snacks and working out doesn't count as training with a weighted vest.

Rule #26
Everyone knows that I'm not a fan of machines for training. But, the #1 machine to avoid at every gym...the vending machine.

Rule #27
Every person should be able to do 6 lifts regardless of age.

Everyone should be able to perform the following lifts (regardless of age): push-ups, inverted rows, squats, deadlifts, split squats (or single-leg elevated squats), and single-leg Romanian deadlifts.

The weight/load, range of motion, implement (piece of equipment), and volume (sets and reps) may vary, but without function in these movements, life is hard.

Thinking I'm talking about a country above and not an exercise is a good sign that you should watch the movements I'm talking about: shelbytrained.com/thecode.

Rule #28
Contrary to popular belief, you invest in personal trainers to help you exercise, not to exercise for you.

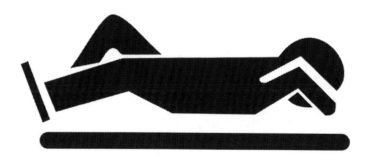

Rule #29
The number one reason females don't look the way they want is that they don't lift weights.

Are you a female? Want to lose more weight? Look better? Be more toned? The answer you love to hate: Increase the weight you're lifting.

The #1 thing I see in females (of any age) trying to improve their body composition (i.e., fat loss) is that they spend too much time worrying about sweating and not enough time worrying about picking up heavier weights.

Think of weights (dumbbells, kettlebells, cables, barbells, etc.) as the engine to power the vehicle: It's much faster and more efficient to get places in the same car (body) but with more horsepower (strength)!

Rule #30
Females don't have to lift "weights" all of the time, but they do need to get stronger.

Functional trainers, stability balls, bands, and bodyweight training have their place in a good training program. The mistake most women make is that they try to "maintain" strength instead of increasing it. I hate to say this, but Mother Nature has other plans for your maintenance – it's called hormones.

Start lifting weights when you're a teenager and don't stop. You'll thank me in your 70s. Worried you'll look like a dude? See Rule #31.

Rule #31
Lifting weights won't make females bulky.

Female Myth: Lifting weights will make you bulky.

Truth: Lifting weights (done properly) will help you not only burn fat, tone your muscles, and increase bone and tendon strength. It will also allow you to keep the weight off without as much effort.

I consider lifting weights for females a lot like an insurance policy: You can get away with a lot more (nutrition and exercise hiccups) if you're picking up heavy things and putting them down.

Know someone who has larger arms than your husband? Either she is using needles other than for sewing or your husband needs to hit the gym.

Rule #32
No one hires me to count their reps. If you're hiring a trainer to help you count your reps, save yourself some money and get a monkey to do it for you.

Rule #33
(Almost) Everyone should still press overhead.

If you've had a shoulder problem, don't ignore overhead pressing. Years ago, I, like many, started to fear overhead work with clients at the risk of creating or increasing shoulder issues. For a few years we avoided almost all overhead work.

What happened? We ended up with more shoulder issues and restrictions as a result of not training a movement that the body is intended to do.

If your shoulder doesn't like going overhead or you're unsure if you should be doing it, give the landmine/lever press a try – it's a great hybrid movement that we use a lot with clients. You can see a video example here: shelbytrained.com/thecode

Rule #34
Gym memberships can be very cost-effective:
If you deduct the cost of TV (cable), internet (wi-fi), and hot water (showers and heat), you're essentially getting paid to work out.

Rule #35
Running doesn't count as leg day.

Running isn't "strength" work for the legs. Your legs fatigue because your body is trying to keep up with blood and oxygen getting to your muscles so that they can contract (and keep you running). Even if running is your sport, putting in a couple days of low-volume strength work will do wonders for your body – and your running!

Rule #36
Train legs at least once a week.

Don't EVER skip legs.

"I want a bigger upper body."

"I already run."

"[Lower-body exercise] hurts my [knees/back/feet], so I don't strength train my lower body."

No matter what your goal is (muscle gain, weight loss, athleticism), training your lower body is your best friend. Sure, the exercise selection, weights, and structure may change, but you need enough in there to support your overall function.

A stronger lower body can do all of those things: help build muscle (even in the upper body), burn fat (even around the mid-section), and improve your speed/quickness/agility (it won't make you muscle-bound).

Rule #37
A great home workout is pushing yourself away from the dinner table. Not only does this help develop upper-body pushing strength, but it can be a great way to reduce caloric intake. Start with 3 sets of 10.

Rule #38
Your push-ups probably need work.

Master the push-up. The push-up is arguably the most-butchered exercise I see performed in any gym – period.

Long before you worry about push-up variations, improve your ability to control your core, your shoulder position/function, and your range of motion.

Three simple tips that help most people:

1) Spread your fingers. Now take your hands/arms and put them out in front of you. Turn your hands/arms to the outside so your index fingers are pointing at 11 and 1 o'clock.

2) Tuck your elbows slightly below shoulder height (toward your torso) when you lower your body.

3) Keep the front side of your pelvis tucked. You can picture a belt buckle on your waist: Flip the belt buckle up toward your ribcage and hold that position.

Now do your push-up. Make sure you move the body as a unit when you lower and raise.

NOTE: See video example: shelbytrained.com/thecode

Rule #39
Your pull-ups are probably friends with your push-ups – and need work.

Pull-ups/chin-ups are probably the second most-butchered exercise I see performed. Just because you can lift your chin up over the bar doesn't mean that you're doing it well. Convulsing and jerking while swinging uncontrollably on the bar is usually a dead giveaway that you need some work.

Below are four tips to help improve pull-ups. (Check out video demonstration: shelbytrained.com/thecode.)

1) Improve your core strength with planks, knee tucks, and other stabilization exercises.

2) Spend more time strengthening your lower and middle traps (prone Ys, wall traces, etc.).

3) Increase the range of motion in your shoulders/lats. One great exercise to do that is the DB Pullover – make sure to keep your ribcage pulled down and your back flat.

4) It's OK to use the lat pull-down machine while you're building up your weaker areas.

Rule #40
Picking up your fork and putting it down 5 times does NOT count as a set of deadlifts.

**Even if it's on the floor and involves multiple plates.*

Rule #41
The rule of half.

How much do you squat? How many chin-ups can you do? Great. Now, take that number and cut it in half.

In a day and age where everyone behind a screen can magically claim weights higher than their incomes, I'm known for keeping people honest. It's not that I don't believe that they've done that many reps or that weight before; it's just that I don't count it if it was done while they were sleeping.

I've seen far too many squats and pull-ups done with subpar form to believe everything I hear. Years ago, one of my athletes told me that he'd done 8 chin-ups as part of his fitness test at school. I put him on the bar right then and there: He did 2 (and a half) full range-of-motion, dead-hang chin-ups.

Rumor also has it that Bigfoot can do pinky pull-ups... I'm calling his bluff and think he probably uses 1-arm instead.

Rule #42
The rule of 2x.

If you already train with me and are wondering how you'll test when you join your team in preseason and if you too should cut your numbers in half, no. It's the exact opposite. Take whatever your numbers are and double them.

I once had a kid take his 135lb front squat to a 330lb back squat for reps in a single day. As much as I would love to sell that type of progress on my 2am infomercials or put them in a bottle at a supplement store, it's simply a matter of making things easier.

The minute you have arbitrary standards on movements, things get out of hand – I mean, I dunked a basketball yesterday in winter boots. What? Does it not count if the hoop was 8 ft?

Rule #43
If you begin to feel lonely while dieting and get the urge to spend some time with your friends and go hang out at the bar, take your friends to the squat rack instead.

Rule #44
Planking for minutes doesn't mean you have a strong core.

Usually it simply means that the ligaments on your spine are tight.

Most planks beyond one minute that I see are no longer being held by the abdominal muscles; instead, the body is "resting" on the ligaments that hold the lumbar spine (lower back) in position.

If you're planking more than a minute, it's time to move on to other progressions or exercises. Take the extra time you save and help solve world hunger.

Rule #45
Doing the agility ladder quickly doesn't mean you've improved your quickness or your foot speed.

It means that you're good at the agility ladder. Unless you're hoping to go to the agility ladder Olympics, spend your time focused on improving the quality of your movement with the ladder. You can effectively train all three types of quickness (positional, reactive, and ground contact) by focusing on landing on the front half of your foot with your heel as close to the ground as possible. As your quality of ground contact improves, you can increase the speed with which you use it.

Rule #46
3 hours can make you a good athlete.

If the average high school athlete asked me how to get more athletic (quicker, faster, stronger, jump higher, etc.) in only 3 hours per week, I'd divide his/her time as follows:

- 30 minutes on mobility/flexibility/warm-up work
- 20 minutes on core/function
- 10 minutes on direct-speed work (sprints, speed techniques, etc.)
- 20 minutes on reactive/plyos (jumping, landing, etc.)
- 1 hour and 40 minutes on functional-strength work (full range-of-motion resistance exercises that challenge single leg/arm, and functional positions).

I could even argue that the athletes should spend much closer to 2+ hours focused on strength work. Most kids simply aren't strong enough to reduce the risk of injury, build muscle, or get faster.

Cardio/Endurance Training:

Rule #47
If you're driving around to find a closer parking space at a gym, remember that many people are paying to walk on a treadmill.

The irony of health and fitness is that people complain about the inconvenience of walking too far in a parking lot, but pay someone to help them improve their physical fitness.

If you're looking for the economical way to improve your cardiovascular health, park really far away from the store.

Next – walk to the sporting good section. You'll have free access to dumbbells, kettlebells, and bands. Hit a

*quick interval-based workout (more on that later —
page 61), then head back to your car.*

*If you're still looking for more, you can always complete
a "finisher" by heading out to the parking lot and
pretending that you can't find your car. Proceed to
walk around the parking lot multiple times looking
really anxious for 5-10 minutes. Watch the fat just
melt away!*

Rule #48
Traditional cardio training shouldn't be your main source of exercise.

If you're trying to maximize your time and results (unless you're a competitive runner):

- Elliptical
- Bike
- Jogging/running

Those 3 exercise options are like hourly-wage employees for your "Healthy Body Business." They will only work when they're "on the clock."

It's not that they don't work; they are just mostly effective during the time you're on them.

Rule #49
Crossing a busy interstate is a great substitute for agility training.

To progress your agility training on a more functional level: Every time a car beeps its horn, change direction. Not only will this work on your auditory skills, but also on your reactive quickness while under pressure.

Rule #50
Shorter is better.

Want more "cardio?" Spend the majority of your time doing short (10-60 seconds of intense periods of exercise), followed by recovery periods of slower exercise.

On top of that you can build in intermediate periods of exercise (2-minute periods), and longer endurance (5+ minutes).

How you put your "cardio" program together is completely up to your goals, likes/dislikes, and time. Most important is to make sure it's something that you can stick with for a period of time without jumping ship to a different and "better" option.

Rule #51
Every exercise can be "cardio."

Anything that gets your heart rate up can be considered "cardio."

Ever done sets of 20 squats? Yeah, I thought so... Still not hard enough? Increase the weight. Still not hard enough? Check to make sure you're not using the Styrofoam weights.

Rule #52
Running from the cops can be a great weekend substitute for sprint intervals.

*Weekdays optional for college kids.

Rule #53
Strength training programs that include sets of 8-15 reps can help endurance.

With a sound training program, a majority of your cardio and endurance training can be done with recreational activities (trail running, hiking, etc.).

Again, the more solid your training program is, the more you can get away with what's fun and enjoyable yet still beneficial!

Rule #54
Avoid trends like the plague.

Any time an entire program is based on one piece of machinery, equipment, or methodology, you should run (not literally). There are hundreds of tools you can do to get a desired result. Depending on your time, goals, level of confidence, etc., you can choose what's right for you.

The last time I checked, digging a hole isn't just "digging a hole." If you were digging a pool or planting a garden, you'd probably use two different tools.

Fitness is no different than digging a hole. Find the right tool(s) for the job.

Rule #55
Economical alternative to elevation training masks: tying a handkerchief around your mouth while training.

Rule #56
The only thing that elevation training masks have been proven to do is make you look like a serial killer.

Hannibal Lecter increased his maximal oxygen update by 53% during a seven-year span while training with a training mask every day.

*Google it if you don't know who he is.

Rule #57
2-minute cardio.

Hate traditional cardio? Or maybe you just want something different? Yeah, me too – we should be friends.

Try this: Set a timer for a desired amount of time (it can vary depending on how much time you have). Pick an exercise or drill to do. Now do as much as you can in the allotted amount of time. A good starting point for time is 2-5 minutes.

Now pick any movement that you can do "well": push-ups, squat jumps, sprints, jumping jacks, spin bike, etc. Start your timer and go.

Want more? Rest one minute, and then repeat. Do this as many times as you need to in order to get your desired result(s).

Rule #58
Walking on a
treadmill works.

Incline walking (treadmill or outside) can be a great complement to traditional strength training. It will not only help overall function, but it is also very low-intensity so recovery isn't an issue (it won't affect your strength training).

As an added bonus, incline walking has been shown to be a valuable tool in weight loss goals for those who are looking for a low-intensity exercise that is easy on them, burns calories, and can be enjoyed with others (family, dogs, etc.).

Rule #59
VO2 Max is useless.

Well, almost. Unless you're an elite endurance athlete (and you're getting paid lots of money to do your sport).

Science has now taught us that VO2 Max (maximum rate of oxygen consumption) isn't nearly as relevant to conditioning as it was once believed.

Want to be in better shape? Want a healthier heart? Want to perform better in your sport? Spend less time trying to push your max (VO2), and spend more time teaching your body to recover between bouts of higher-intensity efforts (exercise). The most effective way to do this is through a variety of high-intensity interval drills or exercises.

Rule #60
Heart rate monitors work.

Heart rate monitoring is the best (and most affordable) way for you techies out there to take a more scientific approach to your conditioning.

If you're doing steady-state, keep your heart rate at about 70-80% of maximum heart rate.

If you're doing interval-based training, allow your heart rate to recover back to about 60-70% of your maximum heart rate.

*If you're not a techie, focus on letting yourself recover until you can talk with normal breath.

Rule #61
Really cold baths are awesome.

I can't call them ice baths, because I typically don't throw ice in mine. What I can tell you is that simply turning the water as cold as it will go and then getting in does amazing things for the body.

How to: Pour ice-cold water; sit in it for 3-8 minutes; and then shower off (with much warmer water).

Fast-forward 12-24 hours and your entire body will be less sore, more vibrant, and refreshed.

Rule #62
Drink lots of water.

The body is made up of 70% water. The risk of consuming too much is very low, and the reward is incredibly high: fullness, weight loss, muscle growth, energy, etc.

You can spend time calculating body weight and hydration levels or you can simply calculate how much you regularly consume and then increase it.

How much? *See Rule #63.

Rule #63
64oz of water per day is a great starting point.

If you exercise and/or are physically active, increase that total to accommodate what you sweat out during your activity. Adjust total water intake from there to your needs based on how you feel and how your body reacts.

We have some people who feel great consuming over 100oz a day, while others tend to feel much better (and visit the bathroom far less) in the 64oz range.

Rule #64
Chasing the ice cream truck doesn't count as "going for a jog around the neighborhood."

As an important follow-up: Eating a large ice cream after exercising doesn't count as a "cone drill" either.

Rule #65
Quality of sleep matters the most.

After years of owning a business, having two kids, and having a spouse do medical school and residency, I've realized that quality matters more than quantity. That's not to say that you'll thrive on 3 hours of quality sleep, but rather than worrying only about the number on the clock, focus on trying to get "better" quality sleep.

A few strategies to start implementing:

1) Stop working on your computer/tablet/phone a couple of hours before you intend to sleep.

2) Spend a couple of minutes focused on breathing, mindfulness, or any strategy that will help slow your heart rate down.

3) Have a routine. The more consistent you are with sleep time, shower, dinner, etc., the better you'll do.

Rule #66
Invest in ME time.

Shoot for 1 hr/week of something non-physically related that you simply enjoy. Chunk it up however you need to fit it into your life: one 60-minute block, twelve 5-minute blocks, five 12-minute blocks. Put away your phone and stay off social media.

If you're new to this concept, start with 15 minutes and work up from there. Make yourself do it no matter how inconvenient it is.

Sometimes that means pulling over onto the side of the road for a few minutes. Sometimes that means giving yourself the "OK" to spend a few minutes doing what you want before tending to other needs.

Trust me, the other needs will still be there in 5 minutes and you'll be much happier.

Rule #67
5 Tips for better sleep.

Five things you should do in a perfect sleep world:

1) Shut off LED devices (blue light) 2 hours prior to sleep. What are LED devices? You know – cell phones, tablets, computers, and TVs.

2) Darken room completely. Wear an eye mask if you need to. I mean, Batman and Zorro both wore masks, right? They were still cool.

3) Turn your room temperature down. There is no magic number, but sticking to your sheets because of sweat won't help.

4) Have a cold shower/bath before getting into bed.

5) Stop consuming caffeine 6-8 hours before bed. This means you should give yourself a cutoff. If you don't have a caffeine-laden beverage by a given time, you skip it – even coffee!

Bonus tip: Exercise regularly.

Nutrition:

Rule #68

Pizza can be a great post-workout treat. Since you'll be at the gym so much, it's important to find ways to still enjoy a nice warm meal.

Pro Tip: Turn on the heated seat in your car to keep the pizza hot while you drive home.

Rule #69
Intermittent fasting life hack: Ignore all "use by" dates on meat.

With more science continuing to support intermittent fasting as an effective option for nutrition, we've tried to support it by bringing new and revolutionary ideas like the above to the masses.

Rule #70
Have no more than 3 dish sizes.

Meal prep can be a game changer. Your ability to prepare meals in advance not only saves time and helps you make better decisions, but it can also help simplify your life and save your "bandwidth."

Start simplifying your life by keeping no more than 3 types of meal prep dishes:

1) Round – for soups and sauce-based meals.

2) Rectangle – for flatter foods.

3) Square – for the in-between foods.

Using only these 3 dishes at every meal (when bringing food for work/school) helps ensure that the volume and structure of your meals is almost identical every time. Fill the dishes the same way each time for a self-regulating calorie counter without having to count calories!

Rule #71
Men should have 50% of their meal as protein.

Men: If you're looking to lean out – have half of your meal composed of lean protein and the other half of vegetables. Follow this 90% of the time and watch the fat get torched.

*No animals were harmed in the making of this rule.

Rule #72
Women should have 1/3 of their meal as protein.

Women: If you want to lose weight, split your meals into ⅔ vegetables and ⅓ lean protein. After that you can worry about fats, fruits, or going keto.

Rule #73
Hitting your macronutrient needs (total caloric intake) is the first thing you should worry about.

Hit that number every day within 50 calories (above or below) and good things will happen. The research on food quality (while convincing) doesn't ever seem to play out in the real world. Get your total caloric intake down, and then start to adjust macronutrients (fat, protein, carbohydrates) and food quality (organic/conventional, etc.).

Do you need to use a scale? Do you need to "count" calories? I don't think you do need to weigh your food or use your calories. But you do need to find a way to quantify your food to make sure you're not overeating – or undereating.

Rule #74
There are 3 important pieces in nutrition.

Three things matter long before anything else:

1. Total food intake (calories)
2. Consistency of timing (same time of day – within a 1-hr window)
3. Consistency of structure (roughly the same size and type of foods each meal).

After that you can start to worry about things like making sure your micronutrients, quality of food, and other pieces are in good shape.

Rule #75
Myth: Your body only needs 60g of protein.

While there are a handful of studies that have shown this, there are also numerous studies indicating that higher intakes (up to 1g/1lb of body weight) do help. Most importantly, we have seen over and over again that people experience better fat loss, energy levels, and performance when they increase their protein intake well beyond 60g.

I once had a female client lose weight (about 40lbs) by increasing her protein intake to approximately 100g per day. After hearing that you could lose weight with less protein, she decreased her protein intake to around 60g per day (same caloric intake). Back came the weight.

Rule #76
It's better to be a 6ft hero than to eat one.

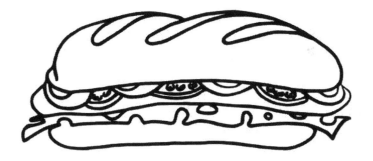

Rule #77
Drink water with every meal to stay full.

Drink water with every meal to help stay full. Sure, there's research that talks about digestion of food and water screwing up that process. However, we've found it much more helpful than hurtful in people's nutrition goals.

Look, if your main issue with nutrition is that you consume water during your meal, email me your phone number and I'll call you with a job offer.

Rule #78
Drink a low-calorie beverage when you're bored.

Drink a flavored beverage (0 or very low-calorie) during quiet times. Seltzer water, tea, flavored water – it doesn't matter what it is as long as it gives you something to do, fills your stomach, and keeps you from consuming useless calories. For me, this act is drinking coffee. It does all of the above, and gives me super powers to run faster, jump higher, and write more workouts. In fact, I put my pants on two legs at a time!

Rule #79
32oz containers rule.

Total fluid intake for people varies, but we tell clients to shoot for a minimum of 64oz over the course of the entire day (not including the water you drank during your workout).

To help keep you on track, split your day into 16hrs of awake time (assuming you sleep 8hrs). Split your 16hrs into (2) 8hr blocks; finish 32oz by the end of your first 8hrs, and then finish the second 32oz by the end of your second 8hrs.

Rule #80
Eating all the junk food in your house doesn't count as "removing all of the bad foods from your cupboards."

Rule #81
Sound nutrition = whole foods + supplements.

Despite what people will tell you, supplements don't cause you to become healthy, lose (or gain) weight, or change your energy. Supplements fill holes in your diet/lifestyle that you can't meet with your current patterns.

Supplements aren't bad. They're just too often misused. Use them where they can help fill a hole in your diet that you can't currently address.

This isn't a free pass to eat like a 12-year-old kid at summer camp. You should always, <u>always,</u> be working to improve your intake of quality whole foods even if you're taking various supplements.

Rule #82
What works for your friends won't necessarily work for you.

Maybe it's easy for them to consume a piece of fruit to increase their vitamin C or halt a sugar craving. However, if you hate peeling oranges, hate the sensation of sticky hands, or need to eat it while driving, it won't work. This is where nutritional strategy comes into play.

Sometimes it may mean adjusting a pattern in your lifestyle. Sometimes it may mean adding a supplement to your diet.

Bottom line: You need to be able to do "it" for it to be effective.

Rule #83
Don't waste your money on most pre-workouts.

Most pre-workouts don't work. Pre-workouts have also been linked to heart murmurs. The tingling sensation you feel is coming from the high levels of vitamin B3 and Niacin. It's called a placebo effect. Enough said.

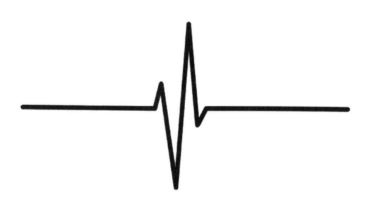

Rule #84
Protein, omega-3s, and greens supplements should be on your radar.

Everyone should look at three supplements: protein, omega-3s, and greens supplements.

Most people don't consume enough protein to meet their physical goals. Most people don't get enough healthy fat in their diets. Most people don't consume a wide enough variety or total intake of vegetables.

I'm not saying that you need all three, or any at all; what I am saying is that many people are guilty of falling short in at least one – if not all three.

Protein will help you keep and build muscle, burn fat, and stay full. It's the only essential macronutrient.

Unless you're eating wild-caught fish every day, you're most likely really low in your omega-3 intake (the healthy fats).

Sure, you may eat a lot of vegetables, but do you really think you're getting the recommended 12 servings? Doubtful (me neither). While greens supplements definitely aren't a replacement for eating vegetables, I consider it a lot like an insurance policy: At least you know you're getting a great deal of the benefits without having to try to eat that much food.

Fat Loss:

Rule #85
If sweating profusely were indicative of a great workout, wool suits, snowsuits, and scarves would be acceptable workout attire.

Rule #86
Myth: You can't turn fat into muscle.

Muscle doesn't replace fat when you work out. Working out effectively causes your body to burn more calories as a source of energy. This (done right) causes your body to use stores of fat for fuel.

If you want to improve how you look, spend the time building muscle from strength training and burn fat from a combination of strength training (lift weights), nutrition (a caloric deficit – less food), and activity (some form of additional caloric expenditure – recreational or otherwise).

Rule #87
10-minute workouts can change your life.

If you're short on time, the best thing you can do is pick four movements that fall into the following four categories:

- Power – jumps, swings, cleans, snatches, etc.
- Lower body – squats, lunges, deadlifts, etc.
- Upper push – push-ups, bench press, overhead press, etc.
- Upper-body pull – pull-up variations, rowing variations

Vary the set and rep scheme from the following: 3, 5, 8, 10, and rotate these 4 movements for as many rounds as possible in a given time period (10 minutes works well). Rest only as needed. Your goal should be 4-6 rounds.

The key here is that you're continually moving from exercise to exercise. Your recovery time for a given muscle group/pattern is when you're training something else. Work hard and move weight and you'll find you can get the body you want in ¼ of the time you had thought you needed.

Rule #88
The elliptical, bike, and treadmill aren't your best friend for fat loss.

Using traditional conditioning-based (cardio) tools to lose fat is like using a wood stove to heat your house: It requires you to keep up the maintenance in order to get the desired results. It's much easier to choose exercises that require the body to burn calories long after you've already done them (in fitness it's often called the Afterburn effect).

It's not that elliptical/bike/jogging don't burn calories (they do); it's just they are not the most efficient use of time for most people.

Rule #89
You can't choose where you lose fat.

Spot reducing fat is almost impossible. Meaning, you can't pick and choose the fat to only come off your abs, or your arms, or your legs.

The good news is that if you are consistent with good training and nutrition, fat will continue to come off for months without making any major changes.

What you can do is increase the muscle tone in a given area to give it better shape while continuing to lose fat throughout your body. If your arms are a problem area, spend more time training your upper body and arms, focusing on getting stronger in the 8-12 rep range. If your legs/hips are the issue, work on improving your squats, deadlifts, and lunges to help create shape while burning calories.

Be patient.

Rule #90
You have abs already.

You already have a six-pack. It's just hidden under a layer (or many) of fat. Unfortunately, while doing a bunch of core work (and crunches) is meant to make your abs look better, no one can see them if you don't lose the fat.

*See above tip for advice on losing abdominal fat.

Rule #91
You're a product of the 5 people you're around the most in the gym.

With all of the research these days talking about you being a by-product of the 5 people you spend the most time with, we've seen a shift in the gym. More and more people are signing up for our group training only to sit there and watch everyone work out.

Contrary to popular belief, you don't lose weight by surrounding yourself with fit people.

Rule #92
Sprints are the
fountain of youth.

Sprints are wondrous for looking and feeling young and keeping your function as a human. Bonus: Sprints are also a great way to stay lean (or get lean).

Rotate your sprints between:
- 10-second max-effort sprints (true sprints) with 50+ seconds of recovery
- 20-40 seconds of sprinting (in a straight line, on a track if possible) with about 40-60 seconds of full recovery
- And 30-60 seconds of sprint intervals going back and forth between two points (typically 10-50 yds), followed by 30-60 seconds of recovery.

Do this 1x/week for health and youthfulness. Do this 2-3x/week for torching fat.

Rule #93
You can hate your life 30 seconds at a time.

Got a bike? Best fat loss workout ever on a bike:

- 30 seconds of work (heavy resistance between 70-85 RPMs or a perceived rate of exertion of an 8), followed by 30 seconds of recovery (easy spin with minimal resistance).
- Do this 20-30 minutes as a stand-alone workout, or 5-15 minutes at the end of a lift (resistance training session).

If you aren't shunning my name with a bunch of expletives after 3 minutes, you're not doing it right.

*Watch the fat literally run away screaming in terror.

Rule #94
Accountability is a must.

Have accountability (pay for it if you need to).

Having someone and/or somewhere to show up helps improve your chance of success by up to as much as 95%! While I'm not sure that a 95% success rate is realistic for most people, I can tell you that it does make a huge difference when you have some form of accountability.

There are tons of options for accountability (apps, friends, significant others, trainers) – it doesn't matter who or what, but having that is key.

Rule #95
Know yourself.

If you can't work out at home, pay for it. A gym membership or personal trainer changes your environment (for the better) and gives you another place to go to help keep the focus and accountability high.

Rule #96
Fact: Telling everyone every time that you work out decreases your caloric expenditure by 23%.

Taking a selfie at the gym before or after your workout nearly doubles that by reducing the caloric expenditure to 41%.

Rule #97
Focus on the process.

Many clients become so engaged in chasing a target goal for weight, body fat percentage, or pants size that they lose sight of the vehicle to actually get them there: the plan.

Keep the daily workout, nutrition, and behaviors as your drivers for success and don't chase the "numbers." Magically, if you're focusing on the right "processes," you'll see good things happen.

Miscellaneous:

Rule #98
Posting on Motivation Mondays doesn't actually move you forward toward any of your goals.

#youhavetoactuallydosomething

Rule #99
The world owes you nothing.

The sooner you realize this, the happier you'll be.

The minute you feel like the amount of effort, money, or desire that you have or have given means you should have a certain outcome, the less likely you are to succeed.

Life is hard. Understand that and realize you must continually work toward what you want. Health, fitness, and performance are no different. To succeed you must show up and pay your dues regularly.

Rule #100
Build people up.

When I was a child, my dad always told me to be nice to people. "You never know when you might need them," he would say. It should go without saying, but in a day and age where people are so immersed in their own world (phones, apps, technology), being a good person and helping people feel good goes a long way.

Rule #101
Don't compare yourself to others.

Comparing yourself to others is a recipe for disaster.

No matter how much weight you lose, how much weight you lift, or how good you eat – there is someone who has lost more, lifts more, or eats better.

Instead of worrying about what they're doing, focus on the variables you can control: yourself and your actions. Find ways to make small daily improvements and you'll continue to make more progress than you ever could have imagined.

Rule #101.01
The Rule of 1%

Small changes in habit and action will change your life.

If you do the math on improving yourself 1% each day for the next 365 days, you'll see exponential growth that is actually 37 times better. If you think of that in terms of health, wellness, or fitness, it's astounding.

What does that mean for you? Spend the time implementing small habits that ultimately create the foundation for long-term success. Do this every day and you'll not only change your life, but you'll start to change those around you.

Final Thoughts

I get paid for results, not for novelty. If you're spinning your wheels or are in a rut where you're making no progress toward your goals, it's time to make a change. Take a step back and analyze what you're doing right now: Is it working? If it isn't, it's time to find a way to create the change you want.

Take the rules in this book and start implementing them one at a time until each one becomes a habit and has been woven into your life. If certain areas need more focus, spend your time there and don't worry about the other ones. If a rule really struck a chord with you, focus on implementing that one rule and ignore the rest.

Lastly, the goal with this book was to create a resource that could be easily read with simple (not easy) actions that you could apply in your own life. If even one rule helps you out, I've done my job.

Here's to a long, healthy, happy life that you can enjoy. Here's to getting #ShelbyTrained!

Client Feedback

The decision to commit to working with Shelby over the past year has turned out to be one of the best choices I could have made regarding my fitness. Having been a runner most of my adult life, I thought I was fairly fit, but had always resisted "weight training." However, I soon discovered that training with Shelby is so much more than that. It has not only helped me to lose the weight gained with transition into mid-life, but also to feel the strongest I have ever felt without injury or sacrificing flexibility or endurance. His experience, thoroughness and encouragement, along with well-thought-out and varying workouts have proved to be invaluable to my overall physical and mental health.
- Dr. Cathy Jakubowitch, Adult – Semi-Private Client

Three things come to mind when I think of Shelby: 1st – Quality. All of the workouts are able to be tailored based on your ability and/or injury. I never worry about injuring myself or doing an exercise. 2nd – I am in the best physical shape of my life. I am an avid runner/hiker and used to have a lot of IT band problems but since I have been training with him, those have gone away. 3rd – Change is good. In all of the years I have been attending class, we have never done the same cycle of exercises. My body/mind definitely responds better to switching things up and this had allowed me to maintain my strength and also helped me improve my running so much! Hills are now my favorite part of the run and cardiovascularly, I am in amazing shape!
- Leslie Durgin, Adult – Group Interval Client

Whether it be quickness or speed, stamina, weight gain, range of motion, etc., he put together numerous plans over the years for myself and other athletes like me. Being a former Division 1 athlete, I can say with certainty that I would not have been able to achieve that level of competition without Shelby.
  - Isaac Lipton, Former Division 1 Lacrosse Player

Shelby's ability to personalize the training regimen to each individual and their needs is the key reason. The second is that the group that trains with Shelby is a good group of people that we have gotten to know, so there is a strong social/community aspect to the group. All trying to improve in our own way using Shelby as the vehicle.
  - George Casey, Adult – Semi-Private Client

I have been training with Shelby Trained for about a year and it has made a huge difference – I am more flexible and my balance is clearly better.
  - Dr. Story Landis, Adult – Semi-Private Client

Why should you consider Shelby to help you achieve your goals? My answer is simple: Few people have the drive, meticulous attention to detail, and desire to innovate that Shelby so effortlessly exudes. There were always bigger gyms with fancier equipment, but of all of the strength coaches I had at my high school and even college, none came close to Shelby's meticulously planned workouts, nutrition plans, and injury prevention methods.
  - Ben Coleman, Former College Baseball Player

Shelby will help you regardless of age, interest, or walk of life. He's a laser-focused, diligent problem solver who sets goals with his clients and strives for results based off of your individual wants and needs! He won't put you in a box you don't fit in and he will constantly change and adapt your programs to help your body work the way you want it to.
- Kellan Humphries, Semi-Private Client

I feel that you have the knowledge, ability and desire to work with each person and their body in a way that would engage them to be the best that they "really" want to be.
- Mary Calvin, Adult – Semi-Private Client

Working with Shelby helped me realize my athletic potential. His training gave me the necessary edge by increasing my vertical and assisting in my speed and agility development to help me reach my goals!
- Stefano Mancini, Former Division 1 Basketball Player

I wouldn't have gained the same confidence in my body without the help and guidance of Shelby and his methods. My only regret was that I wished I had started sooner.
- Olivia Leavitt, Former College Tennis Player

You changed my life forever. Thank you.
- Barbara Charry, Adult – Semi-Private and Group Interval Client

About the Author

Shelby is the owner of Shelby Trained. He's a performance coach and trainer located in Yarmouth, Maine. He has worked with a wide range of clientele from obese and overweight; elderly; kids with various learning disabilities; high school, college, and professional athletes.

Upon graduating with an undergrad degree in Sports Management, Shelby pursued a job as a personal trainer. Shortly after, he obtained his master's degree in Exercise Science. Eventually this led him to blend his love for fitness with business and ultimately it has taken him to where he is today: helping clients improve their lives through positive habit changes.

Shelby believes *success can be yours if you are willing to define it and take the time to build the habits and routines that support it.* That, along with coffee, helps improve your rate of success by 97%.

More information is available at **ShelbyTrained.com**

Other Resources by Shelby Turcotte

If you've enjoyed reading *The Shelby Trained Code,* you'll also love his upcoming book, *Simplementation – The Art and Science of Creating Powerful Change.* Pre-Order is available at: **Simplementationbook.com.**

Interested in hiring Shelby for speaking or consulting for your organization or school?

You can learn more:

Website: shelbytrained.com/consulting

Email: info@shelbytrained.com.

Phone: 207-212-8371

Ways to Get Shelby Trained

- In-Person Semi-Private training for adults
- Group Interval training for adults
- Semi-Private training for athletes
- Small-Group training for athletes
- Group Training for athletes
- Customized Online/Remote Coaching for both adults and athletes
- Group Online/Remote Coaching for both adults and athletes